Pebble Plus

Let's Celebrate

Groundhog Day

FEBRUARY

by Clara Cella

Consulting Editor: Gail Saunders-Smith, PhD

CAPSTONE PRESS
a capstone imprint

Pebble Plus is published by Capstone Press,
1710 Roe Crest Drive, North Mankato, Minnesota 56003.
www.capstonepub.com

Library of Congress Cataloging-in-Publication Data
Cella, Clara.
  Groundhog day / by Clara Cella.
     p. cm. — (Pebble plus. let's celebrate)
  Includes index.
  Summary: "Full-color photographs and simple text provide a brief introduction to Groundhog Day"—Provided
by publisher.
  ISBN 978-1-4296-8731-7 (library binding)
  ISBN 978-1-4296-9386-8 (paperback)
  ISBN 978-1-62065-306-7 (ebook PDF)
  1. Groundhog Day—Juvenile literature. I. Title.

  GT4995.G76C45 2013
  394.261—dc23   2012003827

Editorial Credits

Jill Kalz, editor; Kyle Grenz, designer; Marcie Spence, media researcher; Kathy McColley, production specialist

Photo Credits

AP Images: Keith Srakocic, 11; Bridgeman Art Library: Osterrelchische Galerie Belvedere, Vienna, Austria, 15;
   Capstone Studio: Karon Dubke, 7, 17, 19, 22; Corbis: Jason Cohn/Reuters, 13; iStockphoto: Photawa, cover
   (groundhog); Shutterstock: Antonio S., 5, Bonnie Fink, 9, Miroslav Halama, 1, oliveromg, 21, Smit, cover (green
   tree), Vaclav Volrab, cover (frozen tree)

Note to Parents and Teachers

The Let's Celebrate series supports curriculum standards for social studies related to culture.
This book describes and illustrates the Groundhog Day holiday. The images support early readers
in understanding the text. The repetition of words and phrases helps early readers learn new
words. This book also introduces early readers to subject-specific vocabulary words, which are
defined in the Glossary section. Early readers may need assistance to read some words and to use
the Table of Contents, Glossary, Read More, Internet Sites, and Index sections of the book.

Printed in the United States of America in North Mankato, Minnesota.
042012   006682CGF12

Table of Contents

Hello, Groundhog Day!

Will spring come soon?

Or will winter last longer?

Some people believe

a little animal has the answer.

This animal is a groundhog.

Groundhog Day is February 2. Stories say if a groundhog sees its shadow, winter will last six more weeks. If not, spring will come soon.

A groundhog is a rodent.

It lives in wooded places

and eats plants. A groundhog

can't really tell the weather.

But it's fun to pretend!

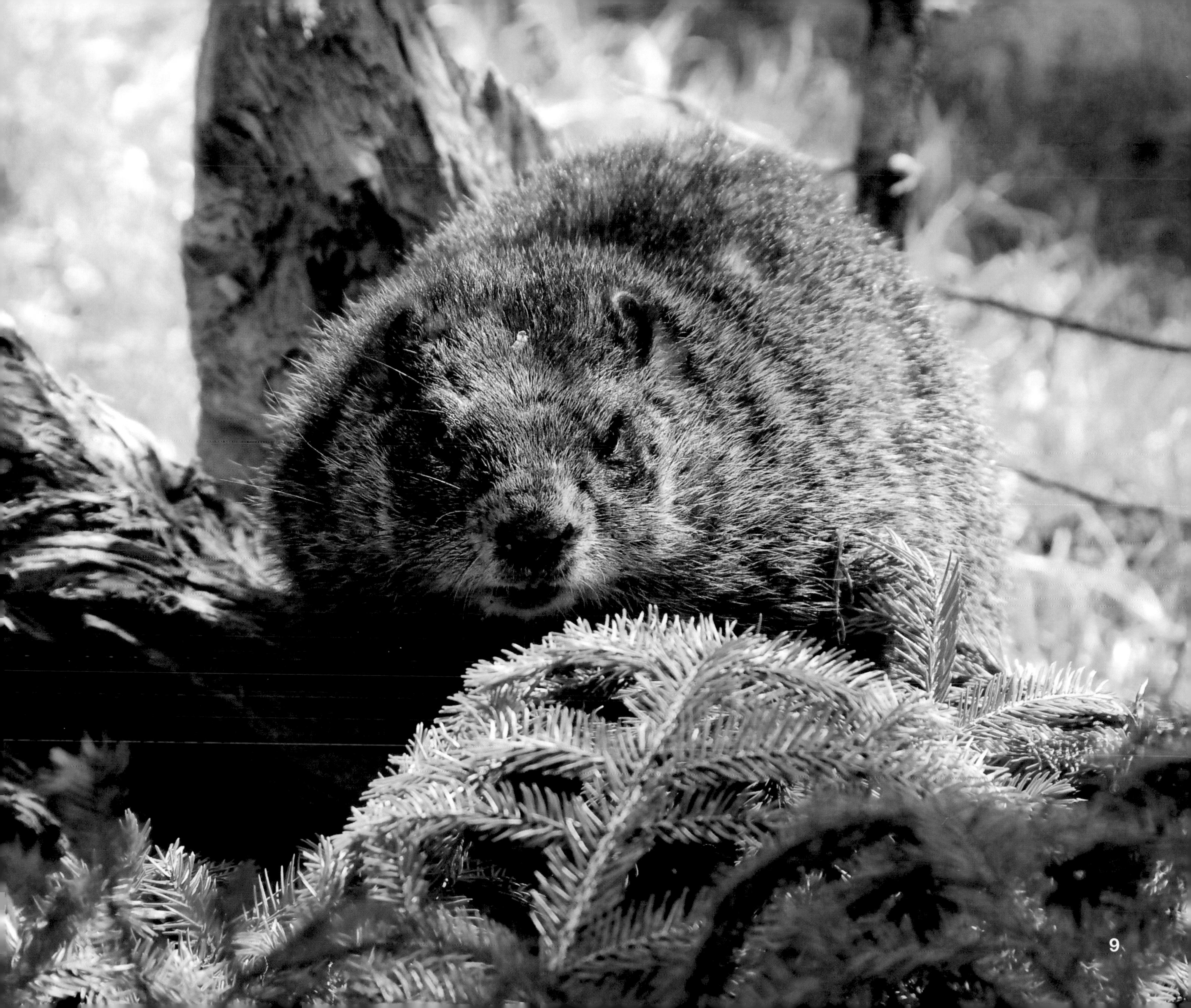

How It Began

Groundhog Day started in 1886. The holiday was first celebrated in Punxsutawney, Pennsylvania. The town groundhog was named Punxsutawney Phil.

Say It Like This

Punxsutawney—punk-suh-TAW-nee

Parts of Groundhog Day come from an old European festival. It was called Candlemas. People watched for signs of spring during Candlemas.

15

Let's Celebrate!

It's Groundhog Day!

How will you celebrate?

Watch Punxsutawney Phil

on TV or on the Internet.

16

Have a party! Some schools have Groundhog Day parties with games and special foods. Wear bright spring colors. Dress up as a groundhog.

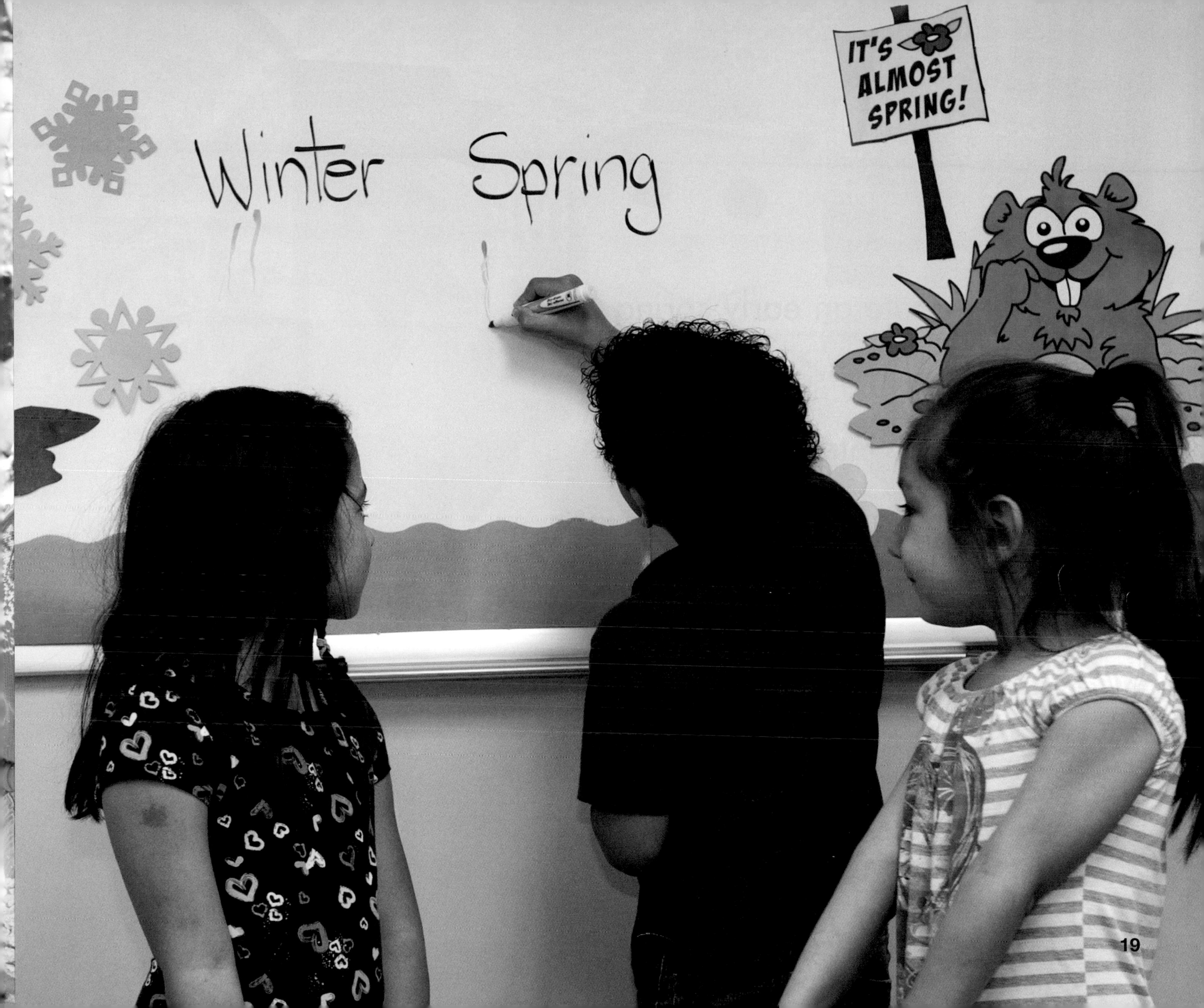
Winter
Spring
IT'S
ALMOST
SPRING!

Activity: Mini Groundhog

Will spring come soon? Pop this groundhog out of its burrow and find out.

What You Need:

brown construction paper

scissors

a glue stick

a black marker

a popsicle stick

a white paper cup

What You Do:

1. Cut out three circles. Make one the size of a quarter, one twice as big, and one half as big.

2. Cut the smallest circle in half (ears).

3. Glue the halves to the middle-size circle (head). Then glue the middle-size circle to the big circle (body).

4. Draw eyes, a nose, a mouth, and whiskers.

5. Glue the groundhog to the top of the popsicle stick.

6. Make a slit in the bottom of the cup. Slide the popsicle stick through. Move the stick to move your groundhog!

Read More

Gibbons, Gail. *Groundhog Day!* New York: Holiday House, 2007.

Peppas, Lynn. *Groundhog Day.* Celebrations in My World. New York: Crabtree Pub. Co., 2010.

Phillips, Dee. *Groundhog's Burrow.* The Hole Truth! — Underground Animal Life. New York: Bearport Pub., 2012.

Internet Sites

FactHound offers a safe, fun way to find Internet sites related to this book. All of the sites on FactHound have been researched by our staff.

Here's all you do:

Visit *www.facthound.com*

Type in this code: 9781429687317

Super-cool stuff!

Check out projects, games and lots more at
www.capstonekids.com

Glossary

burrow—a tunnel or hole in the ground made or used by an animal

Candlemas—an old European festival to welcome spring that was held on February 2

celebrate—to honor someone or something on a special day

rodent—a mammal with long front teeth used for gnawing; rats, mice, and squirrels are rodents

Index

Word Count: 197
Grade: 1

Early-Intervention Level: 18